ORIGIN OF THE GREAT DANE

That the Great Dane is an ancient breed is not difficult to prove. Although many breed books attempt to cite Old World artwork, documents, sculpture and other artifacts as definite proof of a breed's authenticity, the presence of a Great Dane-like dog in ancient Egypt and eventually in the country now known as Germany cannot be disputed. A Great Dane-like dog cuts a fairly specific image and it has been claimed that drawings of such dogs can be found on Egyptian monuments dating back as far as several thousand years B.C. Likewise, coins that were struck before the birth of Christ depict likenesses of this dog. Also there is a fascinating engraving

Three hundred years ago the famous Dutch artist Van Dyck painted the Duke Wolfgang William v. Neuberg with a Great Dane, which resembles very much the type we know today.

done in the late 17th century that portrays likely Great Dane ancestors participating in a boar hunt!

What does the boar have to do with the Great Dane?, you ask. The Great Dane was once known as the Boar Hound! Not a very attractive name, and nowhere as noble as the name we use today—although the breed may be "Great", we know for certain he doesn't hail from Denmark. So there might be something rotten there, after all....

The Great Dane's beginnings as a hunter of boar explains one very important and today controversial aspect of the breed's history: his cropped ears. Unless you've seen pictures of a Great Dane with natural, dropped ears, as is the standard in England and Australia for example, you'd never guess that this noble head has ears belonging to the hound family. Those very ears, long and pendant, were a problem for a boar hunter, as the wild pigs could latch on to them and rip them. Therefore, the style of cropping the ears and setting them to stand erect came to be. The Germans are given credit for the origination of the cropped-ear style. From the paintings that we have seen of a boar hound crop, it was strictly utilitarian and hardly stylized as the ears were short, ugly and triangular. Today, the Dane ear is cropped longer and appears more graceful and balanced to the head size, beautifully complementing the dog's head piece.

There is much debate over the cropping of ears as the English and Australians have outlawed the practice. In America and Canada, however, aesthetics and style are not the sole reasons for cutting the ears, although they are admittedly the main reasons. Arguably, the cropped ear is a canker-free ear and none of the difficulties of the long-eared dog such as split or sore ends occurs. Experienced breeders and veterinarians in the United States commonly crop puppies' ears at around six weeks. Look at photographs of dogs with dropped ears and cropped ears, see which style appeals to you. In the U.S., many breeders are beginning to show dogs with natural ears, and some judges are even favoring these dogs over the cropped-ear dogs.

The history of the breed also reflects the color of the dogs. As with all breeds, different colors come in and out of favor. Today the fawn Great Dane is perhaps the most popular, though many prefer the harlequin (black and white) or the brindles.

In years past, the brindles were called Ulmar Doggen, the fawns were named Danische Doggen, and the harlequins were called Tiger Doggen. There is some debate as to why the Germans called the harlequin "Tiger Dog". Perhaps they were envisioning the Siberian Tiger, which is black and white, if not patterned like a Dane, or perhaps, as some historians state, they were referring to the tiger horse, which is of white coloration with small black spots.

After many names were employed over the years, such as Hatzrude, Saufanger, and Metzgerhund, the German breeders formally adopted the official name of Deutsche Dogge, making it the national dog of Germany in the latter half of the 19th century.

How the translation to English of Deutsche Dogge (meaning German Dog) became Great Dane, as he is known in America and the British Empire, is a confusing matter. Perhaps it was simply the incorrect translation of "Deutsche", as was the case with the Pennsylvania Dutch community, who were actually Pennsylvania "Deutsche" (German). Regardless, no one has been able to come up with any definitive explanation.

The Great Dane in England can

be traced back over two hundred years. There is historical record of English Great Danes around 1775, tying into art records, paintings, and tapestries of Dane-like dogs. All we know for certain, however, is what we find in the pedigrees. Americans imported the greatest number of Danes from Germany, despite England's headstart and consistent quality. In the years prior to World War II, American breeders purchased many, many fine German Great Danes, and our pedigrees today trace back to these imports. In truth, there are few top dogs in Washington, and Wisconsin. The English Great Dane club was founded four years before that, and the German club two years later. The Great Dane Club of America, by the way, was only the fourth breed club to become a member of the American Kennel Club. When admitted to membership, it was known as the Great German Mastiff Club.

The Philadelphia show (1877) was just seven years prior to the first recorded event of English Great Danes in 1884. In this case the dogs were actually shown as Grand Danes and Boar Hounds.

During the latter half of the 19th century in Germany, Great Danes were given the official name of Deutsche Dogge and were made the national dog of that country. Pictured are Wurtemberg Great Danes of the 1880s.

America today who do not have a German import in their pedigree.

In the late 19th century in Philadelphia, one dog show recorded 13 dogs entered as Siberian or Ulm dogs. These are believed to be the first Great Danes shown in America. In 1886, the first Great Dane club was organized in Chicago with 33 members from all parts of the country—California, Illinois, Iowa, Kansas, Montana, New York, These dogs did not look like the massive and grand specimens we see gracing our show rings today. By no means. Photographs from 1840 to the end of that century show us dogs that are shockingly small with coarse heads, and unimpressive necks and bodies. There are some dogs pictured that exhibit little body mass and are entirely too fine, also with weak heads. All dogs possessed ears that were cut extremely short and

The original boar hound crop was strictly utilitarian and hardly stylized as ears were short, ugly, and triangular. This photograph dates back to about 1890.

graceless. The elegance and grandeur of today's Dane are entirely accomplishments of the 20th century. Breeders of today must be credited for transforming those inelegant creatures of the past into the miraculous and massive animals that we know today as Great Danes.

DESCRIPTION OF THE BREED

From the organization of the first American Great Dane Club in 1886 until the present year, our breed has flourished to the extent that our show points are among the highest due to our huge entries at the shows. Current Great Dane breeders can be, for the most part, very proud of their breeding. They are making every effort to produce a near-to-the-standard dog. "Near to the standard" is the closest any breeder can hope to come to the perfect animal. Absolute perfection, in any living thing, is an impossibility. The flawless human has yet to be born. The flawless pup has yet to be whelped in any breed—including ours.

All the Dane's fine qualities should be housed in a good "bred to standard" Great Dane body. The Great Dane standard, produced and distributed by the Great Dane Club of America, is the bible of all the constructive Great Dane breeders. In it, for example, are listed the accepted colors of Great Danes for the show ring. They are: fawn, brindle, harlequin, black, and blue. All colors should have dark brown eyes. Light eyes or two different colors are permitted in a harlequin, but are not desirable. Fawns and brindles should be enhanced with dark masks.

The desired shade in fawns is a rich golden—not buff or brown. The brindle has strong black stripings on a golden base color. The harlequin should be pure white with jet black torn patches irregularly and well distributed over the entire body. Pure white neck and front legs are preferred. The blue is a pure steel blue, as far as possible without any suggestion of yellow, black, or mouse-gray. (The mouse-gray Great Dane, sometimes mistakenly called a blue, is often

ISABELLE FRANCAIS

On a harlequin Great Dane, a pure white neck and front legs are preferred.

This is a beautiful headstudy of the Best of Breed winner of the 1994 Westminster Kennel Club dog show, Ch. Longo's Sweetalk V Michaeldane. Owners, Joe and Tootie Longo.

ISABELLE FRANCAIS

STANDARD FOR THE BREED

A breed standard is the criterion by which the appearance (and to a certain extent, the temperament as well) of any given dog is made subject to objective measurement. Basically, the standard for any breed is a definition of the perfect dog, to which all specimens of the breed are compared. Breed standards are always subject to change through review by the national breed club for each dog, so it is always wise to keep up with developments in a breed by checking the publications of your national kennel club.

The Great Dane combines dignity and elegance with great size.

ISABELLE FRANCAIS

OFFICIAL AKC STANDARD FOR THE GREAT DANE

General Appearance—The Great Dane combines, in its regal appearance, dignity, strength and elegance with great size and a powerful, well-formed, smoothly muscled body. It is one of the giant working breeds, but is unique in that its general conformation must be so well balanced that it never appears clumsy, and shall move with a long reach and powerful drive. It is always a unit—the Apollo of dogs. A Great Dane must be spirited, courageous, never timid; always friendly and dependable. This physical and mental combination is the characteristic that gives the Great Dane the majesty possessed by no other breed. It is particularly true of this breed that there is an impression of great masculinity in dogs, as compared to an impression of femininity in bitches. Lack of true Dane breed type, as defined in this standard, is a serious fault.

length is in proportion to the size of the head and the ears are carried uniformly erect. **Nose** shall be black, except in the blue Dane, where it is dark blue-black. A black spotted nose is permitted in the harlequin, a pink colored nose is not desirable. A split nose is a disqualification. **Teeth** shall be strong, well developed, clean and with full dentition. The incisors of the lower jaw touch very lightly the bottoms of the inner surface of the upper incisors (scissors bite). An undershot jaw is a very serious fault. Overshot or wry bites are serious faults. Even bites, misaligned or crowded incisors are minor faults.

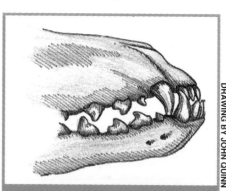

Undershot bite. An under jaw appreciably longer than the upper one and frequently turned up as well, resulting in a bite in which the lower incisors erupt well in front of those in the upper jaw.

DRAWING BY JOHN QUINN

Neck, Topline, Body—The neck shall be firm, high set, well arched, long and muscular. From the nape, it should gradually broaden and flow smoothly into the withers. The neck underline should be clean. Withers shall slope smoothly into a short level back with a broad loin. The chest shall be broad, deep and well muscled. The forechest should be well developed without a pronounced sternum. The brisket extends to the elbow, with well sprung ribs. The body underline should be tightly muscled with a well-defined tuck-up. The croup should be broad and very slightly sloping. The tail should be set high and smoothly into the croup, but not quite level with the back, a continuation of the spine. The tail should be broad at the base, tapering uniformly down to the hock joint. At rest, the tail should fall straight. When excited or running, it may curve slightly, but never above the level of the back. A ring or hooked tail is a serious fault. A docked tail is a disqualification.

Forequarters—The forequarters, viewed from the side, shall be strong and muscular. The shoulder blade must be strong and sloping, forming, as near as possible, a right angle in its articulation with the upper arm. A line from the upper tip of the shoulder to the back of the elbow joint should be perpendicular. The ligaments and muscles holding the shoulder blade to the rib cage must be well developed, firm and securely attached to prevent loose shoulders. The shoulder blade and the upper arm should be the same length. The elbow should be one-half the distance from the withers to the ground. The strong pasterns should slope slightly. The feet should be round and compact with well-arched toes, neither toeing in, toeing out, nor rolling to the inside or outside. The nails should be short, strong and as dark as possible, except that they may be lighter in harlequins. Dewclaws may or may not be removed.

Hindquarters—The hindquarters shall be strong, except they may be lighter in harlequins. Wolf claws are a serious fault.

Coat—The coat shall be short, thick and clean with a smooth, glossy appearance.

Color, Markings and Patterns— *Brindle*—The base color shall be yellow gold and always brindled with strong black cross stripes in a chevron pattern. A black mask is preferred. Black should appear

ROBERT SMITH

In the harlequin Great Dane, the base color is pure white with black torn patches irregularly and well distributed over the entire body.

muscular, broad and well angulated, with well let down hocks. Seen from the rear, the hock joints appear to be perfectly straight, turned neither toward the inside nor toward the outside. The rear feet should be round and compact, with well-arched feet, toeing neither in nor out. The nails should be short, strong and as dark as possible, on the eye rims and eyebrows, and may appear on the ears and tail tip. The more intensive the base color and the more distinct and even the brindling, the more preferred will be the color. Too much or too little brindling are equally undesirable. White markings at the chest and toes, black-fronted, dirty colored brindles are not desirable.

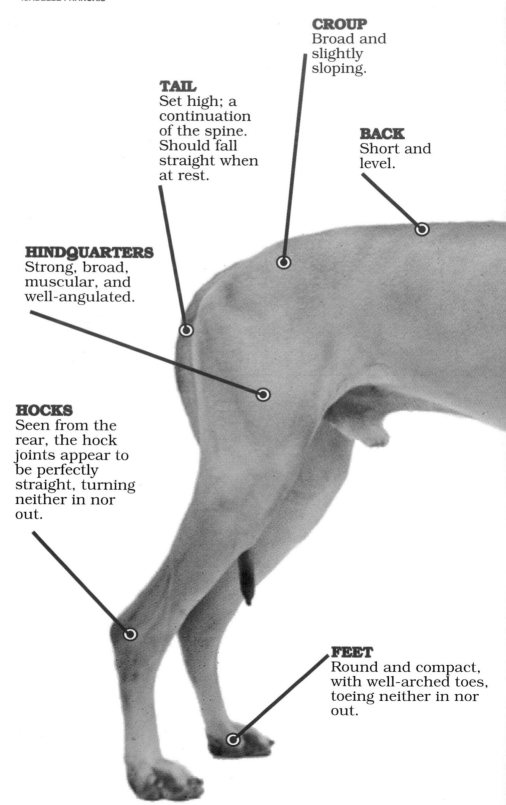

1995 Westminster Kennel Club Best of Breed winner
Ch. Terregan's Magic Show owned by Terri Loncrini.

CROUP
Broad and
slightly
sloping.

TAIL
Set high; a
continuation
of the spine.
Should fall
straight when
at rest.

BACK
Short and
level.

HINDQUARTERS
Strong, broad,
muscular, and
well-angulated.

HOCKS
Seen from the
rear, the hock
joints appear to
be perfectly
straight, turning
neither in nor
out.

FEET
Round and compact,
with well-arched toes,
toeing neither in nor
out.

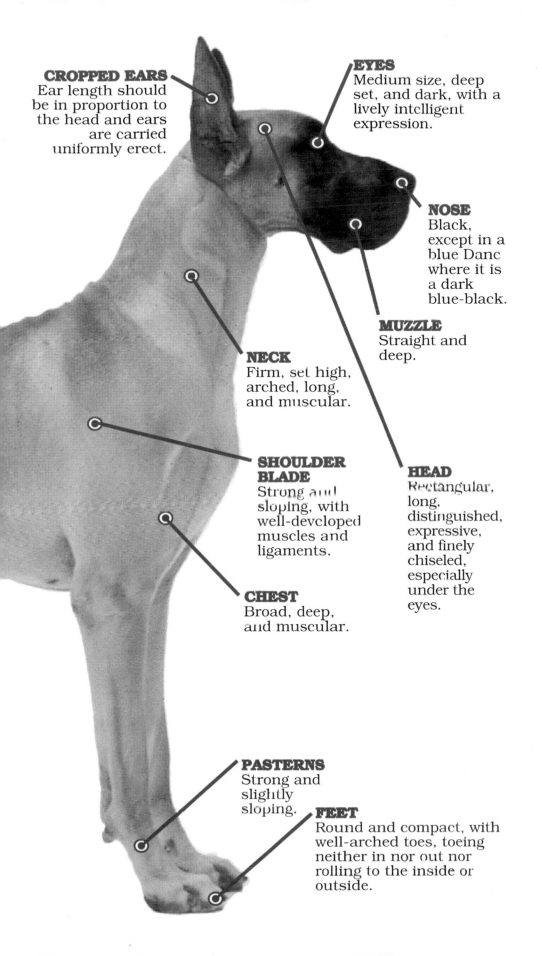

CROPPED EARS
Ear length should
be in proportion to
the head and ears
are carried
uniformly erect.

EYES
Medium size, deep
set, and dark, with a
lively intelligent
expression.

NOSE
Black,
except in a
blue Dane
where it is
a dark
blue-black.

MUZZLE
Straight and
deep.

NECK
Firm, set high,
arched, long,
and muscular.

**SHOULDER
BLADE**
Strong and
sloping, with
well-developed
muscles and
ligaments.

HEAD
Rectangular,
long,
distinguished,
expressive,
and finely
chiseled,
especially
under the
eyes.

CHEST
Broad, deep,
and muscular.

PASTERNS
Strong and
slightly
sloping.

FEET
Round and compact, with
well-arched toes, toeing
neither in nor out nor
rolling to the inside or
outside.

DRAWING BY JOHN QUINN

The mask is dark shading of varying degrees about the head forming a mask-like pattern. In the Great Dane the mask encompasses the muzzle region.

Blue—The color shall be a pure steel blue. White markings at the chest and toes are not desirable. ***Black***—The color shall be a glossy black. White markings at the chest and toes are not desirable.

Harlequin—Base color shall be pure white with black torn patches irregularly and well distributed over the entire body; a pure white neck is preferred. The black patches should never be large enough to give the appearance of a blanket, nor so small as to give a stippled or dappled effect. Eligible, but less desirable, are a few small gray patches, or a white base with single black hairs showing through, which tend to give a salt and pepper or dirty effect. *Any variance in color or markings as described above shall be faulted to the extent of the deviation. Any Great Dane which*

The gait of the Great Dane denotes strength and power with long, easy strides. The backline should appear level and parallel to the ground.

ISABELLE FRANCAIS

ROBERT SMITH

The Great Dane is spirited, courageous, friendly, and dependable.

does not fall within the above color classifications must be disqualified.

Gait—The gait denotes strength and power with long, easy strides resulting in no tossing, rolling or bouncing of the topline or body. The backline shall appear level and parallel to the ground. The long reach should strike the ground below the nose while the head is carried forward. The powerful rear drive should be balanced to the reach. As speed increases, there is a natural tendency for the legs to converge toward the centerline of balance beneath the body. There should be no twisting in or out at the elbow or hock joints.

Temperament—The Great Dane must be spirited, courageous, always friendly and dependable, and never timid or aggressive.

DISQUALIFICATIONS
Danes under minimum height.
Split nose.
Docked tail.
Any color other than those described under "Color, Markings and Patterns."

This is Ch. West Wind Always Tomorrow, a fawn Great Dane. Note the black mask.

ISABELLE FRANCAIS

GREAT DANE TEMPERAMENT

Great Danes, often called the Apollos of dogdom, have, through the years, been beloved house dogs of all classes and types of people from the obscure to the famous. Great Danes are large and for those of us who own them, the larger the better.

dogs are often considered to be too big to be more than a watch dog or a dog to be kept at a distance because of its size. This is very wrong. A Great Dane can be a wonderful companion, friend and a pleasure as well as a guardian of all, young and old. We

ROBERT SMITH

Although considered a giant in the dog world, the Great Dane is so well behaved and reserved that size should not be a deterrent to owning one.

They are so well-behaved and reserved, however, that their size is no deterrent to owning a Great Dane, even in a small home. These dogs will adjust happily to whatever quarters are provided by their new owner. Every new owner should know that the Great Dane needs love and human companionship. These gentle

believe the most important thing you can give your Great Dane is love and companionship. You will find that he will return it a thousand-fold.

It is a misconception that Great Danes require estate-sized living quarters or a huge exercising area. It is also often said that a mature member of the breed has a daily meat bill so high only a millionaire could pay it. What could be less true? Rather these majestic dogs ornament a palace with the same grace and poise as a toy living in a modest home and the small wallet can afford to feed a Great Dane without undue strain.

The Great Dane is a family dog for children—with his inborn patience and understanding.

Great Dane traits and characteristics are the same as those found in a very nice human being. A well-bred and happy dog of this breed has dignity, loyalty, a sense of humor, and is always companionable. A Great Dane has a vast amount of tolerance

ISABELLE FRANCAIS

The Great Dane is a perfect pet for children—he is gentle, affectionate, patient, and protective.

dog. He does not readily or quickly accept strangers. The loud, fierce-sounding bark is excellent insurance against intruders. The Great Dane is a man's dog. He is big, fast, powerful, and courageous. The Great Dane is a woman's dog. He is gentle, affectionate, and protective. And what a wonderful

for the vagaries of human nature, and an infinite capacity for sympathy. We had a death in the family of a loved one, far from where we were living. As we sat stunned by the news of a telegram, one of the Danes came over, put his big head on a sagging shoulder, and tried to kiss away the falling tears.

YOUR NEW GREAT DANE PUPPY

SELECTION

When you do pick out a Great Dane puppy as a pet, don't be hasty; the longer you study puppies, the better you will understand them. Make it your transcendent concern to select only one that radiates good health and spirit and is lively on his feet, whose eyes are bright, whose coat shines, and who comes forward eagerly to make and to cultivate

DOCUMENTS

Now, a little paper work is in order. When you purchase a purebred Great Dane puppy, you should receive a transfer of ownership, registration material, and other "papers" (a list of the immunization shots, if any, the puppy may have been given; a note on whether or not the puppy has been wormed; a diet and feeding schedule to which the

Selecting your Great Dane puppy can be difficult, especially from this adorable lot; pick the puppy that picks you!

your acquaintance. Don't fall for any shy little darling that wants to retreat to his bed or his box, or plays coy behind other puppies or people, or hides his head under your arm or jacket appealing to your protective instinct. *Pick the Great Dane puppy who forthrightly picks you! The feeling of attraction should be mutual!*

puppy is accustomed) and you are welcomed as a fellow owner to a long, pleasant association with a most lovable pet, and more (news)paper work.

GENERAL PREPARATION

You have chosen to own a particular Great Dane puppy. You have chosen it very carefully over all other breeds and all other puppies. So before you ever get that Great Dane puppy home, you will have prepared for its arrival by reading everything you can get your hands on having to do with the management of Great Danes and puppies. True, you will run into many conflicting opinions, but at least you will not be starting "blind." Read, study, digest. Talk over your plans with your veterinarian, other "Great Dane people," and the seller of your Great Dane puppy.

Choose a Great Dane puppy with bright eyes and a clean, shiny coat!

ISABELLE FRANCAIS

When you get your Great Dane puppy, you will find that your reading and study are far from finished. You've just scratched the surface in your plan to provide the greatest possible comfort and health for your Great Dane; and, by the same token, you do want to assure yourself of the greatest possible enjoyment of this wonderful creature. You must be ready for this puppy mentally as well as in the physical requirements.

TRANSPORTATION

If you take the puppy home by car, protect him from drafts, particularly in cold weather. Wrapped in a towel and carried in the arms or lap of a passenger, the Great Dane puppy will usually make the trip without mishap. If the pup starts to drool and to squirm, stop the car for a few minutes. Have newspapers handy in case of car-sickness. A covered carton lined with newspapers provides protection for puppy and car, if you are driving alone. Avoid excitement and unnecessary handling of the puppy on arrival. A Great Dane puppy is a very small "package" to be making a complete change of surroundings and company, and he needs frequent rest and refreshment to renew his vitality.

THE FIRST DAY AND NIGHT

When your Great Dane puppy arrives in your home, put him down on the floor and don't pick him up again, except when it is absolutely necessary. He is a dog,

Whether solid black or harlequin, with lots of love and attention your Great Dane will grow into a truly wonderful canine companion.

The longer you study Great Dane puppies, the better you will understand them and the easier it will be to choose one.

ISABELLE FRANCAIS

Remember that a new puppy is like a child and needs constant care and supervision.

ISABELLE FRANCAIS

with soap and water, wipe up the floor and dry it well. Then take the wet paper and place it on a fairly large square of newspapers in a convenient corner. When cleaning up, always keep a piece of wet paper on top of the others. Every time he wants to "squat," he will seek out this spot and use the papers. (This routine is rarely necessary for more than three days.) Now leave your Great Dane puppy for the night. Quite probably he will cry and howl a bit; some are more stubborn than others on this matter. But let him stay alone for the night. This may seem harsh treatment, but it is the best procedure in the long run. Just let him cry; he will weary of it sooner or later.

easily cleaned. Let him explore the kitchen to his heart's content; close doors to confine him there. Prepare his food and feed him lightly the first night. Give him a pan with some water in it—not a lot, since most puppies will try to drink the whole pan dry. Give him an old coat or shirt to lie on. Since a coat or shirt will be strong in human scent, he will pick it out to lie on, thus furthering his feeling of security in the room where he has just been fed.

HOUSEBREAKING HELPS

Now, sooner or later—mostly sooner—your new Great Dane puppy is going to "puddle" on the floor. First take a newspaper and lay it on the puddle until the urine is soaked up onto the paper. *Save this paper.* Now take a cloth

These partners in crime will soon be separated. Puppies learn a lot of important lessons from their littermates.

ISABELLE FRANCAIS

Great Danes just love the great outdoors!

EXERCISE AND ENVIRONMENT

The mature Great Dane does not need as much exercise as is commonly supposed. We have heard that a member of this breed must have a 2-5 mile walk every day to maintain health. We also understand that a Great Dane a mature Great Dane keeps him in the house as a member of the family. As such, the dog goes upstairs, downstairs, and in and out of rooms, many times a day. That is exercise—ask any housewife. If you live in an apartment you will need

Daily exercise will benefit your Great Dane both physically and mentally.

ROBERT SMITH

belonging to a man who owns a horse is in a very fortunate situation! The dog then can take a daily cross-country run following the rider on his pace-setting horse. This would be a good idea—if Great Danes wore shoes—or needed such violent exercise.

We assume that the owner of to walk your Dane about 2 miles, dividing it into four trips daily.

For fresh-air running and "duty doing," a fenced 25 by 40 foot space is adequate. The fence should be 5 to 6 feet high. If you have an enclosed area, regardless of size, keep it clean. The runs can be

These young Danes are enjoying a friendly game of tug-of-war. Two dogs can be good company for one another, if you have the means and room to take care of them.

enclosed with chain-link fencing, and cement- or cinder-floored, if money is no object. Equally safe, if pennies must be counted, is a 5- or 6-foot high hogwire fence fastened to cedar posts. The good earth is the floor.

Environment covers a lot of territory. Again, we assume that the Great Dane is a member of the family. All the humans have beds; the dog is entitled to one also. A comfortable 4-foot by 4-foot quilted or foam rubber pad with some sort of washable cover is ideal. Or more economical, cedar shavings in a washable denim bag of adequate size is more than satisfactory. In case this sounds like pampering the dog

Great Danes are playful and always appreciate a roll in the grass on a sunny day—the perfect opportunity for a tummy rub!

Engaging in playful activity with your Great Dane is a good form of exercise for both you and your dog as well as a perfect opportunity to bond.

ISABELLE FRANCAIS

too much, remember that a Great Dane must have something soft on which to lie. Otherwise, because of the weight of the animal, he develops large unsightly callouses on the elbows. Shoe boils (bursitis) may also develop.

The dog's bed should be in a warm, dry, draft-free place; never, never in the cellar where it is too often damp, a sure invitation to arthritis and other diseases of the joints. A bed and fresh water at all times are essential for your dog.

Although there is a lot of dog to cover, the Great Dane's short coat is easy to care for, requiring little more than a quick once-over.

GROOMING

Despite the Great Dane's enormous size, grooming him is a cinch! Albeit there's a lot of dog to cover, the coat itself requires little more than a quick once-over. Unlike many other breeds, there is no stripping, plucking, or shaping required by a professional groomer.

With just weekly brushings, the Great Dane coat can be kept immaculately clean. Of all dogs, the Dane is among the most odor-free. A rubber horse curry and a brush helps to remove dust and loose hair. On the off chance that your Dane has managed to soil his coat, cleaning pads with witch hazel or alcohol and water sponged on the dog do the trick. Pet shops offer better options in the way of coat preparations, conditioners and of course specially designed dog shampoos. These products last a long time, are generally concentrated, and are fairly inexpensive.

Pet shops offer a wide variety of combs and brushes. For the Great Dane a large slicker brush is virtually all that is needed. Photo courtesy of Hagen.

In general, however, Great Danes need not be bathed on a regular basis. Many believe only when absolutely necessary. Given the size of the dog and how wet you're going to get giving the bath, there's no reason to undertake this feat too often. When you do bathe your dog, make sure that you use cleansing preparations specifically formulated for use on dogs. The ears are cleaned with alcohol on cotton swabs. Work carefully but thoroughly all around the inside of the ear to remove the oily dirt that accumulates there, but never poke or dig into the ear canal.

The care of a Great Dane's nails from early puppyhood should be constant, as it is so important. The ideal foot for this breed is cat-like, highly arched, and tightly closed. Unless the nails are kept as short as possible, the dog goes back on his feet to prevent his overly long nails from striking the ground.

Since many dogs are very sensitive about having their feet touched in the first place, it is advisable to establish the nail-clipping routine as early as possible. The nails need to be cut periodically so as to avoid the quick, the vein in each nail, from growing so near the surface that it is impossible to get the nails short. If you cut the quick, your Dane will let you know as the nail will bleed and it is painful for the dog. If this happens, he will become fearful of the nail cutter. A dog who doesn't like his feet touched and then has a painful experience will be a terror the next time you try to cut his nails. The mere

When you bathe your Great Dane, be sure to use a shampoo made especially for dogs. Human shampoos are usually too harsh and can irritate your dog's skin. Photo courtesy of Hagen.

Keeping your Great Dane's ears clean is simple if you use a top-quality lotion. Be careful to never poke or dig into the ear canal. Photo courtesy of Hagen.

sight of the clipper can send your Dane into a frenzy to escape the oncoming discomfort.

On a practical note, if a nail is cut too short and bleeds, we suggest Monsels (ferric subsulfate) salts or powdered styptic be pressed on the cut edge. This will stop the bleeding, though it may not calm your upset Dane down right away.

Adult Danes should have their nails trimmed about every three weeks. If the dog is walked on pavement as opposed to run on grass, his nails will likely need less trimming. Puppies are more unpredictable as their nails grow variably from dog to dog. Simply watch the feet and keep the nails trim so that they do not extend beyond the foot.

Don't ever forget your Dane's teeth. They require regular attention as tartar forms on the

ISABELLE FRANCAIS

Although your Great Dane does not need to be bathed frequently, he should be rinsed off thoroughly after swimming.

teeth and must be removed. Accumulated tartar can do irreparable damage to the tooth and be just the start of major health problems. The veterinarian can show you how to brush and even scale your Dane's teeth. We cannot emphasize enough that the teeth be kept clean throughout a dog's life. This will make for sweeter breath and a healthier dog. Without adequate attention, a dog will more than likely lose his teeth prematurely. Owners must provide their dogs with safe chew products in addition to their veterinary visits. Nylabone® products are the safest and the ones recommended by most veterinarians. Look for them in pet shops and pet-supply houses.

It is easy to groom your Great Dane. A handsome Great Dane is a wondrous creature and who would dream of not keeping him looking his dramatic best— squeaky clean and glistening with good health.

ISABELLE FRANCAIS

Your Great Dane should always have access to fresh, cool water, especially when outdoors. Although these friendly Danes are sharing, your dog should have his own bowl.

FEEDING

A Great Dane should always be fed and watered at shoulder height. Because of their long legs they should be fed "high," as they say for dogs. Exceptions, of course, are puppies.

Feeding stands can be bought, but this is not necessary. A kitchen stool with a home-made guard around the top to hold the dish secure, a wide kitchen sill, or, for a young Dane, a kitchen chair are all of good height for feeding. Stainless steel or aluminum pans are most satisfactory as they are so easy to keep clean. Now let's talk about feeding your Great Dane, a subject so simple that it's amazing there is so much nonsense and misunderstanding about it. Is it expensive to feed a Great Dane? No, it is not! You can feed your Great Dane economically and keep him in perfect shape the year round, or you can feed him expensively. He'll thrive either way, and let's see why this is true.

First of all, remember a Great Dane is a dog. Dogs do not have a high degree of selectivity in their food, and unless you spoil them with great variety (and possibly turn them into poor, "picky" eaters) they will eat almost anything that they become accustomed to. Many dogs flatly refuse to eat nice, fresh beef. They pick around it and eat everything else. But meat—bah! Why? They aren't accustomed to it! They'd eat rabbit fast enough, but they refuse beef because they aren't used to it.

Don't let your Great Dane pick up scraps that may be unsafe and unsanitary to gnaw on. Provide him with safe chew toys, such as a Nylabone®, to satisfy his chewing needs.

ROBERT SMITH

VARIETY NOT NECESSARY

A good general rule of thumb is forget all human preferences and don't give a thought to variety.

Choose the right diet for your Great Dane and feed it to him day after day, year after year, winter and summer. But what is the right diet?

Hundreds of thousands of dollars have been spent in canine nutrition research. The results are conclusive, so you needn't go into a lot of experimenting with trials of this and that every other week. Research has proven just what your dog needs to eat and to keep healthy.

DOG FOOD

There are almost as many right diets as there are dog experts, but the basic diet most often recommended is one that consists of a dry food, either meal or kibble form. There are several of excellent quality, manufactured by reliable companies, research tested, and nationally advertised. They are inexpensive, highly satisfactory, and available in stores everywhere in containers of five to 50 pounds. Larger amounts cost less per pound, usually.

If you have a choice of brands, it is usually safer to choose the

Great Danes will do anything for a treat!

ISABELLE FRANCAIS

better known one; but even so, carefully read the analysis on the package. Do not choose any food in which the protein level is less than 25 percent, and be sure that this protein comes from both animal and vegetable sources. The good dog foods have meat meal, fish meal, liver, and such, plus protein from alfalfa and soy beans, as well as some dried-milk product. Note the vitamin content carefully. See that they are all there in good proportions; and be especially certain that the food contains properly high levels of vitamins A and D, two of the most perishable and important ones. Note the B-complex level, but don't worry about carbohydrate and mineral levels. These substances are plentiful and cheap and not likely to be lacking in a good brand.

The advice given for how to choose a dry food also applies to moist or canned types of dog foods, if you decide to feed one of these.

Having chosen a really good food, feed it to your Great Dane as the manufacturer directs. And once you've started, stick to it. Never change if you can possibly help it. A switch from one meal or kibble-type food can usually be made without too much upset; however, a change will almost invariably give you (and your Great Dane) some trouble.

WHEN SUPPLEMENTS ARE NEEDED

Now what about supplements of various kinds, mineral and vitamin, or the various oils? They are all okay to add to your Great Dane's food. However, if you are feeding your Great Dane a correct diet, and this is easy to do, no supplements are necessary unless your Great Dane has been improperly fed, has been sick, or is having puppies. Vitamins and minerals are naturally present in all the foods; and to ensure against any loss through processing, they are added in concentrated form to the dog food you use. Except on the advice of

A Great Dane from Willowdane Kennels enjoys a Nylabone®.

VINCE SERBIN

your veterinarian, added amounts of vitamins can prove harmful to your Great Dane! The same risk goes with minerals.

FEEDING SCHEDULE

When and how much food should you give your Great Dane? As to when (except in the instance of puppies), suit yourself. You may feed two meals per day or the same amount in one single feeding, either morning or night. As to how to prepare the food and how much to give, it is generally best to follow the directions on the food package. Your own Great Dane may want a little more or a little less.

Fresh, cool water should always be available to your Great Dane. This is important to good health throughout his lifetime.

ALL GREAT DANES NEED TO CHEW

Puppies and young Great Danes need something with resistance to chew on while their teeth and jaws are developing—for cutting the puppy teeth, to induce growth

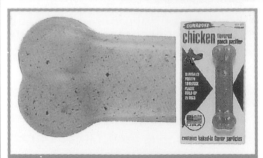

A chicken-flavored Gumabone® has tiny particles of chicken powder embedded in it to keep your Great Dane interested.

of the permanent teeth under the puppy teeth, to assist in getting rid of the puppy teeth at the proper time, to help the permanent teeth through the gums, to ensure normal jaw development, and to settle the permanent teeth solidly in the jaws.

The adult Great Dane's desire to chew stems from the instinct for tooth cleaning, gum massage, and jaw exercise—plus the need for an outlet for periodic doggie

Pet shops sell real bones that have been colored, cooked, dyed, or served natural. Some of the bones are huge, but they are usually easily destroyed by Great Danes and can become very dangerous.

tensions.

This is why dogs, especially puppies and young dogs, will often destroy property worth hundreds of dollars when their chewing instinct is not diverted from their owner's possessions. And this is why you should provide your Great Dane with something to chew—something that has the necessary functional qualities, is desirable from the Great Dane's viewpoint, and is safe for him.

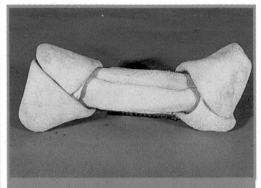

Rawhide is probably the best-selling dog chew. It can be dangerous and cause a dog to choke on it as it swells when wet. A molded, melted rawhide mixed with casein is available (though always scarce). This is the only suitable rawhide for Great Danes.

It is very important that your Great Dane not be permitted to chew on anything he can break or on any indigestible thing from which he can bite sizable chunks. Sharp pieces, such as from a bone which can be broken by a dog, may pierce the intestinal wall and kill. Indigestible things that can be bitten off in chunks, such as from shoes or rubber or plastic toys, may cause an intestinal stoppage (if not regurgitated) and bring painful death, unless surgery is promptly performed.

Strong natural bones, such as 4- to 8-inch lengths of round shin bone from mature beef—either the kind you can get from a butcher or one of the variety available commercially in pet stores—may serve your Great Dane's teething needs if his mouth is large enough to handle them effectively. You may be tempted to give your Great Dane puppy a smaller bone and he may not be able to break it when you do, but puppies grow rapidly and the power of their jaws constantly increases until maturity. This means that a growing Great Dane may break one of the smaller bones at any time, swallow the pieces, and die painfully before you realize what is wrong.

All hard natural bones are very abrasive. If your Great Dane is an avid chewer, natural bones may wear away his teeth prematurely; hence, they then should be taken away from your dog when the teething purposes have been served. The badly worn, and usually painful, teeth of many mature dogs can be traced to excessive chewing on natural bones.

Contrary to popular belief, knuckle bones that can be chewed up and swallowed by your Great Dane provide little, if any, usable calcium or other nutriment. They do, however, disturb the digestion of most dogs and cause them to vomit the nourishing food they need.

Dried rawhide products of various types, shapes, sizes, and prices are available on the market and have become quite popular. However, they don't serve the primary chewing functions very well; they are a bit messy when wet from mouthing, and most Great Danes chew them up rather rapidly but they have been considered safe for dogs until recently. Now, more and more incidents of death, and near death, by strangulation have been reported to be the results of

The Nylabone®/Gumabone® Pooch Pacifiers enable the dog to slowly chew off the knobs while they clean their own teeth. The knobs develop elastic frays which act as a toothbrush. These pacifiers are extremely effective as detailed scientific studies have shown.

partially swallowed chunks of rawhide swelling in the throat. More recently, some veterinarians have been attributing cases of acute constipation to large pieces of incompletely digested rawhide in the intestine.

A new product, molded rawhide, is very safe. During the process, the rawhide is melted and then injection molded into the familiar dog shape. It is very hard and is eagerly accepted by Great Danes. The melting process also sterilizes the rawhide. Don't confuse this with pressed rawhide, which is nothing more than small strips of rawhide squeezed together.

The nylon bones, especially those with natural meat and bone fractions added, are probably the most complete, safe, and economical answer to the chewing need. Dogs cannot break them or bite off sizable chunks; hence, they are completely safe—and being longer lasting than other things offered for the purpose, they are economical.

Hard chewing raises little bristle-like projections on the surface of the nylon bones—to provide effective interim tooth cleaning and vigorous gum massage, much in the same way your toothbrush does it for you. The little projections are raked off and swallowed in the form of thin shavings, but the chemistry of the nylon is such that they break down in the stomach fluids and pass through without effect.

The toughness of the nylon provides the strong chewing resistance needed for important jaw exercise and effectively aids teething functions, but there is no tooth wear because nylon is non-abrasive. Being inert, nylon does not support the growth of microorganisms; and it can be washed in soap and water or it can be sterilized by boiling or in an autoclave.

Nylabone® is highly recommended by veterinarians as a safe, healthy nylon bone that can't splinter or chip. Nylabone® is frizzled by the dog's chewing action, creating a toothbrush-like surface that cleanses the teeth and massages the gums. Nylabone®, the only chew products made of flavor-impregnated solid nylon, are available in your local pet shop. Nylabone® is superior to the cheaper bones because it is made of virgin nylon, which is the strongest and longest-lasting type of nylon available. The cheaper bones are made from recycled or re-ground nylon scraps, and have a tendency to break apart and split easily.

Nothing, however, substitutes for periodic professional attention for your Great Dane's teeth and gums, not any more than your toothbrush can do that for you. Have your Great Dane's teeth cleaned at least once a year by your veterinarian (twice a year is better) and he will be happier, healthier, and far more pleasant to live with.

Most pet shops have complete walls dedicated to safe pacifiers.

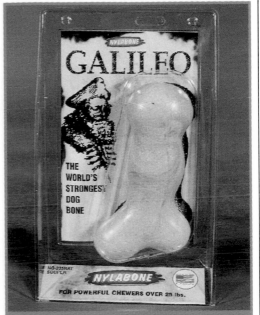

The Galileo is an extremely tough nylon pacifier. Its design is based upon original sketches by Galileo Galilei Linceo. A booklet explaining the history and workings of the design come in each package. This might very well be the best design for the Great Dane.

Great Danes have such strong jaws that most ordinary chew devices are quickly destroyed. The Hercules™ has been designed with the Great Dane and other hard-biting large breeds in mind. It is made of polyurethane, like your car bumper, but is more appealing.

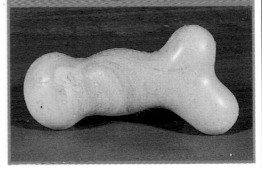

Raised dental tips on each dog bone work wonders with controlling plaque in Great Danes.

Only buy the largest Plaque Attacker™ for your Great Dane!

Because he is such a large animal, basic obedience training is a must for the Great Dane.

TRAINING

All dogs should be well-trained and live under firm but kind discipline. For a Great Dane that sentence changes from should to must. A mature dog of this breed is well aware of his size and power. He is, consequently, fearless. Unless trained, such a large animal will not be a satisfactory house pet.

You owe proper training to your Great Dane. The right and privilege of being trained is his birthright; and whether your Great Dane is going to be a handsome, well-mannered housedog and companion, a show dog, or whatever possible use he may be put to, the basic training is always the same—all must start with basic obedience, or what might be called "manner training."

Your Great Dane must come instantly when called and obey the "Sit" or "Down" command just as fast; he must walk quietly at "Heel," whether on or off lead. He must be mannerly and polite wherever he goes; he must be polite to strangers on the street and in stores. He must be mannerly in the presence of other dogs. He must not bark at children on roller skates, motorcycles, or other domestic animals. And he must be restrained from chasing cats. It is not a dog's inalienable right to chase cats, and he must be reprimanded for it.

Retractable leashes are the preferred type for Great Danes. The Trakt enables you to adjust the length of the leash. Photo courtesy of Hagen.

PROFESSIONAL TRAINING

How do you go about this training? Well, it's a very simple procedure, pretty well standardized by now. First, if you can afford the extra expense, you may send your Great Dane to a professional trainer, where in 30 to 60 days he will learn how to be a "good dog." If you enlist the services of a good professional trainer, follow his advice of when to come to see the dog. No, he won't forget you, but too-frequent visits at the wrong time may slow down his training progress. And using a "pro" trainer means that

is to join an obedience training class right in your own community. There is such a group in nearly every community nowadays. Here you will be working with a group of people who are also just starting out. You will actually be training your own dog, since all work is done under the direction of a head

After you have finished training your Great Dane for basic obedience, you can begin to teach him other tasks, such as fetching a newspaper.

you will have to go for some training, too, after the trainer feels your Great Dane is ready to go home. You will have to learn how your Great Dane works, just what to expect of him and how to use what the dog has learned after he is home.

OBEDIENCE TRAINING CLASS

Another way to train your Great Dane (many experienced Great Dane people think this is the best)

trainer who will make suggestions to you and also tell you when and how to correct your Great Dane's errors. Then, too, working with such a group, your Great Dane will learn to get along with other dogs. And, what is more important, he will learn to do exactly what he is told to do, no matter how much confusion there is around him or how great the temptation is to go his own way.

Write to your national kennel

VINCE SERBIN

"Sit" is one of the basic obedience commands you will need to teach your Great Dane.

club for the location of a training club or class in your locality. Sign up. Go to it regularly—every session! Go early and leave late! Both you and your Great Dane will benefit tremendously.

TRAIN HIM BY THE BOOK

The third way of training your Great Dane is by the book. Yes, you can do it this way and do a good job of it too. But in using the book method, select a book, buy it, study it carefully; then study it some more, until the procedures are almost second nature to you. Then start your training. But stay with the book and its advice and exercises. Don't start in and then make up a few rules of your own. If you don't

follow the book, you'll get into jams you can't get out of by yourself. If after a few hours of short training sessions your Great Dane is still not working as he should, get back to the book for a study session, because it's your fault, not the dog's! The procedures of dog training have been so well systemized that it must be your fault, since literally thousands of fine Great Danes have been trained by the book.

After your Great Dane is "letter perfect" under all conditions, then, if you wish, go on to advanced training and trick work.

Your Great Dane will love his obedience training, and you'll burst with pride at the finished product! Your Great Dane will enjoy life even more, and you'll enjoy your Great Dane more. And remember—you *owe good training to your Great Dane.*

SUCCESSFUL DOG TRAINING is one of the better dog training books by Hollywood dog trainer Michael Kamer, who trains dogs for movie stars.

A handler is the person who is at the human end of the leash while the dog is in the show ring. Much of this Great Dane's performance in the show ring is dependent upon the experience and the know-how of his handler.

SHOWING YOUR GREAT DANE

A show Great Dane is a comparatively rare thing. He is one out of several litters of puppies. He happens to be born with a degree of physical perfection that closely approximates the standard by which the breed is judged in the show ring. Such a dog should, on maturity, be able to win or approach his championship in good, fast company at the larger shows. Upon finishing his championship, hc is apt to be as highly desirable as a breeding animal. As a proven stud, he will automatically command a high price for service.

Showing Great Danes is a lot of fun—yes, but it is a highly competitive sport. While all the experts were once beginners, the odds are against a novice. You will be showing against experienced handlers, often people who have devoted a lifetime to breeding, picking the right ones, and then showing those dogs through to their championships. Moreover,

In the show ring, gait is an important part of conformation competition. It is a reliable indicator of how soundly constructed the animal is. The Great Dane should move with a long, easy, springy stride, with no tossing or rolling of the body.

ISABELLE FRANCAIS

the most perfect Great Dane ever born has faults, and in your hands the faults will be far more evident than with the experienced handler who knows how to minimize his Great Dane's faults. These are but a few points on the sad side of the picture.

The experienced handler, as I say, was not born knowing the ropes. He learned—*and so can you!* You can if you will put in the same time, study and keen observation that he did. But it will take time!

KEY TO SUCCESS

First, search for a truly fine show prospect. Take the puppy home, raise him by the book, and as carefully as you know how, give him every chance to mature into the Great Dane you hoped for. My advice is to keep your dog out of big shows, even Puppy Classes, until he is mature. Maturity in the male is roughly two years; with the female, 14 months or so. When your Great Dane is approaching maturity, start out at match shows, and, with this experience for both of you, then go gunning for the big wins at the big shows.

Next step, read the standard by which the Great Dane is judged. Study it until you know it by heart. Having done this, and while your puppy is at home (where he should be) growing into a normal, healthy Great Dane, go to every dog show you can possibly reach. Sit at the ringside and watch Great Dane judging.

The handler's job is to make sure that their dog is always being seen to its best advantage.

Keep your ears and eyes open. Do your own judging, holding each of those dogs against the standard, which you now know by heart.

In your evaluations, don't start looking for faults. Look for the virtues—the best qualities. How does a given Great Dane shape up against the standard? Having looked for and noted the virtues, then note the faults and see what prevents a given Great Dane from standing correctly or moving well. Weigh these faults against the virtues, since, ideally, every feature of the dog should contribute to the harmonious whole dog.

"RINGSIDE JUDGING"

It's a good practice to make notes on each Great Dane, always holding the dog against the standard. In "ringside judging," forget your personal preference for this or that feature. What does the standard say about it? Watch carefully as the judge places the dogs in a given class. It is difficult from the ringside always to see why number one was placed over the second dog. Try to follow the judge's reasoning. Later try to talk with the judge after he is finished. Ask him questions as to why he placed certain Great Danes and not others. Listen while the judge explains his placings, and, I'll say right here, any judge worthy of his license should be able to give reasons.

When you're not at the ringside, talk with the fanciers and breeders who have Great Danes. Don't be afraid to ask opinions or say that you don't know. You have a lot of listening to do, and it will help you a great deal and speed up your personal progress if you are a good listener.

THE NATIONAL CLUB

You will find it worthwhile to join the national Great Dane club and to subscribe to its magazine. From the national club, you will learn the location of an approved regional club near you. Now, when your young Great Dane is eight to ten months old, find out the dates of match shows in your section of the country. These differ from regular shows only in that no championship points are given. These shows are especially

your Great Dane is always being seen to its best advantage. The other job is to keep your eye on the judge to see what he may want you to do next. Watch only the judge and your Great Dane. Be quick and be alert; do exactly as the judge directs. Don't speak to him except to answer his questions. If he does something you don't like, don't say so. And don't irritate the judge (and everybody else) by

Before you begin showing your Great Dane, it is a good idea to go to shows and watch other Great Danes being judged.

ISABELLE FRANCAIS

designed to launch young dogs (and new handlers) on a show career.

ENTER MATCH SHOWS

With the ring deportment you have watched at big shows firmly in mind and practice, enter your Great Dane in as many match shows as you can. When in the ring, you have two jobs. One is to see to it that

constantly talking and fussing with your dog.

In moving about the ring, remember to keep clear of dogs beside you or in front of you. It is my advice to you *not* to show your Great Dane in a regular point show until he is at least close to maturity and after both you and your dog have had time to perfect ring manners and poise in the match shows.

Your Great Dane should always be a picture of health—with a shiny, smooth coat, clear eyes, and a moist nose.

ISABELLE FRANCAIS

YOUR HEALTHY GREAT DANE

Your Great Dane is as picturesque and imposing as Apollo himself: a walking sculpture of good health: vibrant, rich colors, shiny, smooth coat, clear eyes, pink gums, moist nose, and ever-alert and responsive. We know our pets, their moods and habits, and therefore we can recognize when our Great Dane is experiencing an off-day. Signs of sickness can be very obvious or very subtle. As any mother can attest, diagnosing and treating an ailment requires common sense, knowing when to seek home remedies and when to visit your doctor, or veterinarian, as the case may be.

Your veterinarian, we know, is your Great Dane's best friend, next to you. It will pay to be choosy about your veterinarian. Talk to dog owning friends whom you respect. Visit more than one vet before you make a lifelong choice. Trust your instincts. Find a knowledgeable, compassionate vet who knows Great Danes and likes them.

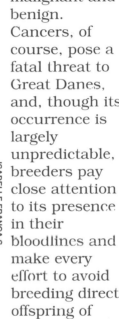
ISABELLE FRANCAIS

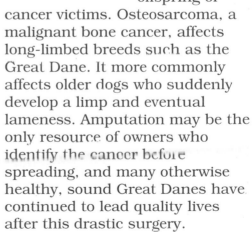
Puppies should generally be vaccinated at 12 weeks of age and then annually.

MAJOR HEALTH ISSUES

Among the most pressing health concerns of Great Dane breeders and owners today is cancer as the breed has shown a high incidence of tumors, both malignant and benign. Cancers, of course, pose a fatal threat to Great Danes, and, though its occurrence is largely unpredictable, breeders pay close attention to its presence in their bloodlines and make every effort to avoid breeding direct offspring of cancer victims. Osteosarcoma, a malignant bone cancer, affects long-limbed breeds such as the Great Dane. It more commonly affects older dogs who suddenly develop a limp and eventual lameness. Amputation may be the only resource of owners who identify the cancer before spreading, and many otherwise healthy, sound Great Danes have continued to lead quality lives after this drastic surgery.

The Great Dane's heart presents problems in many bloodlines. Among the heart problems from which the Great Dane suffers are cardiomyopathy, heart murmur, heart tumors, and subaortic stenosis. The form of cardiomyopathy that affects Great Danes is known as dilated cardiomyopathy (DCM). It is commonly seen in large breeds, and usually isn't identifiable until three or four years of age. In this disease the heart muscles become thin and the heart is unable to pump correctly, ultimately leading to heart failure. Signs of the disease include an increased heart rate, unusual intolerance for exercise, difficulty breathing, coughing and general depression.

Bloat, also known as gastric dilation-volvulus syndrome (GDV), is a tragic condition that affects large, deep-chested breeds such as the Great Dane. A life-threatening condition, GDV is caused by aerophagia, swallowing air that causes the stomach to be distended. Air gulping is a result of stress, vigorous exercise or bolting of food or water. Bloat implies that the flow of stomach fluid has been completely obstructed, resulting in the organ twisting. The stomach is distended by gas build-up and is forced to twist on its axis, blocking all entry and exit. Unless the condition is detected immediately and treated vigorously, the dog will go into shock, suffer from clotting abnormalities and/or heart failure, and often die.

Prevention of bloat requires the understanding that feeding one large meal a day to a large dog is very dangerous: feed two to three smaller meals each day. Also never allow the dog to consume

Your Great Dane should always have time to catch his breath. Never allow him to participate in overly vigorous exercise or play.

ISABELLE FRANCAIS

Whether puppy or adult, your Great Dane should be maintained through regular visits to the veterinarian.

large amounts of water at one time, and never over-exercise a large dog.

Panosteitis affects large and giant breeds through inflammation of the leg bones. Affected dogs, more often male, experience lameness which moves from leg to leg. The condition is described as self-limiting, sets in around four to eight months of age and is nearly always self-cured by two years of age, often as early as one year. Anti-inflammatory drugs help in severe cases where the dog is experiencing pain; otherwise there is no specific treatment.

Another disease of the leg bones and their development is hypertrophic osteodystrophy, which also affects young growing dogs around four months of age. It is characterized by a painful swelling of the joints. Little definite is known about the disease, including whether it is genetically passed. Some veterinarians purport that a vitamin C imbalance may be responsible, though supplementation is never advised. Others blame an infection, though no organism yet has been identified. Anti-inflammatories help, as does cage rest.

Hypothyroidism, a common endocrine disorder in dogs, is difficult to diagnose but has some incidence in the Great Dane. The thyroid can be affected by any of a number of other diseases, such as diabetes, liver and kidney disease, heart failure, etc. Skin problems, hair loss, lack of appetite, and sex hormone imbalance can all affect the thyroid, making hypothyroidism ever more evasive for a veterinarian to identify positively. Modern veterinary research, however, can assist in thyroid-hormone replacement and other treatments that can help affected dogs.

The Great Dane's eyes are fairly sensitive and require delicate care. Although the breed is not plagued by eye problems, owners should be aware of the occurrence of cataracts in certain Dane lines.

Wobbler syndrome, known also as spondylolithesis or cervical vertebral instability, affects the neck disks of Great Danes. Rear quarter incoordination is a recognizable sign of the syndrome. Surgery promises some success for Wobbler syndrome provided that no permanent spinal-cord damage has been sustained.

Many Great Danes are predisposed to certain congenital and inherited abnormalities, such as hip dysplasia, a blatantly

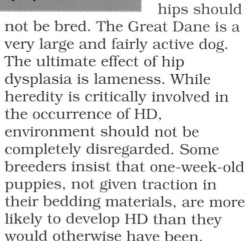

During outdoor activity, your Great Dane should take time out to rest his muscles and bones so as to avoid any injuries.

common problem in purebred dogs with few exceptions. Ask the breeder for records of any of these problems before acquiring a puppy.

Hip dysplasia deserves special attention by Great Dane people. This congenital hip malformation can involve the absolute dislocation of the hip or simply a bad fit into the socket. The condition is present at birth but may take five to six months to a few years to manifest. All dogs should be x-rayed for the presence of hip dysplasia. Dogs who show bad hips should not be bred. The Great Dane is a very large and fairly active dog. The ultimate effect of hip dysplasia is lameness. While heredity is critically involved in the occurrence of HD, environment should not be completely disregarded. Some breeders insist that one-week-old puppies, not given traction in their bedding materials, are more likely to develop HD than they would otherwise have been.

ANAL SACS

An owner must pay special attention to anal sacs, sometimes called anal glands, which are

This is Kennesaw's Dane Astro, CGC. The title CGC means that this dog has passed the Canine Good Citizen Test, which promotes responsible dog ownership and good canine members of society.

ISABELLE FRANCAIS

located in the musculature of the anal ring, one on either side. Each empties into the rectum via a small duct. Occasionally their secretion becomes thickened and accumulates so you can readily feel these structures from the outside. If your Great Dane is scooting across the floor dragging his rear quarters, or licking his rear, his anal sacs may need to be expressed. Placing pressure in and up toward the anus, while holding the tail, is the general routine. Anal sac secretions are characteristically foul-smelling, and you could get squirted if not careful. Veterinarians can take care of this during regular visits and demonstrate the cleanest method.

VACCINATIONS

For the continued health of your dog, owners must attend to vaccinations regularly. Your veterinarian can recommend a vaccination schedule appropriate for your dog taking into consideration the factors of climate and geography. The basic vaccinations to protect your dog are: parvovirus, distemper, hepatitis, leptospirosis, adenovirus, parainfluenza, coronavirus, bordetella, tracheobronchitis (kennel cough), Lyme disease and rabies.

Parvovirus is a highly contagious, dog-specific disease, first recognized in 1978. Targeting the small intestine, parvo affects the stomach and diarrhea and vomiting (with blood) are clinical signs. Although the dog can pass the infection to other dogs within three days of infection, the initial signs, which include lethargy and depression, don't display themselves until four to seven days. When affecting puppies under four weeks of age, the heart muscle is frequently attacked. When the heart is affected, the puppies exhibit difficulty in breathing and experience crying and foaming at the nose and mouth.

Distemper, related to human measles, is an airborne virus that spreads in the blood and ultimately in the nervous system and epithelial tissues. Young dogs or dogs with weak immune systems can develop encephalomyelitis (brain disease) from the distemper infection. Such dogs experience seizures, general weakness and rigidity, as well as "hardpad". Since distemper is largely incurable, prevention through vaccination is vitally important. Puppies should be vaccinated at six eight weeks of age, with boosters at ten to 12 weeks. Older puppies (16 weeks and older) who are unvaccinated should receive no fewer than two vaccinations at three to four week intervals.

Hepatitis mainly affects the liver and is caused by canine adenovirus type I. Highly infectious, hepatitis often affects dogs nine to 12 months of age. Initially the virus localizes in the dog's tonsils and then disperses to the liver, kidney and eyes. Generally speaking the dog's immune system is capable of combating this virus. Canine infectious hepatitis affects dogs whose systems cannot fight off the adenovirus. Affected dogs have fever, abdominal pains, bruising on mucous membranes and gums, and experience coma and convulsions. Prevention of hepatitis exists only through vaccination at eight to ten weeks of age and then boosters three or four weeks later, then annually.

Leptospirosis is a bacterium-related disease, often spread by rodents. The organisms that spread leptospirosis enter through the mucous membrane and spread to the internal organs via the bloodstream. It can be passed through the dog's urine. Leptospirosis does not affect young dogs as consistently as the other viruses; it is reportedly regional in distribution and somewhat dependent on the immunostatus of the dog. Fever, inappetence, vomiting, dehydration, hemorrhage, kidney and eye disease can result in moderate cases.

Bordetella, called canine cough, causes a persistent hacking cough in dogs and is very contagious. Bordetella involves a virus and a bacteria: parainfluenza is the most common virus implicated;

Bordetella bronchiseptica, the bacterium. Bronchitis and pneumonia result in less than 20 percent of the cases, and most dogs recover from the condition within a week to four weeks. Non-prescription medicines can help relieve the hacking cough, though nothing can cure the condition before it's run its course. Vaccination cannot guarantee protection from canine cough, but it does ward off the most common virus responsible for the condition.

Lyme disease (also called borreliosis), although known since for decades, was only first diagnosed in dogs in 1984. Lyme disease can affect cats, cattle, and horses, but especially people. In the U.S., the disease is transmitted by two ticks carrying the *Borrelia burgdorferi* organism: the deer tick (*Ixodes scapularis*) and the western black-legged tick (*Ixodes pacificus*), the latter primarily affects reptiles. In Europe, *Ixodes ricinus* is responsible for spreading Lyme. The disease causes lameness, fever, joint swelling, inappetence, and lethargy. Removal of ticks from the dog's coat can help reduce the chances of Lyme,

An adorable pair of Great Dane puppies.

ISABELLE FRANCAIS

though not as much as avoiding heavily wooded areas where the dog is most likely to contract ticks. A vaccination is available, though has not been proven to protect dogs from all strains of the organism that causes the disease.

Rabies is passed to dogs and

Vaccinations are strongly recommended as affected dogs are too dangerous to manage and are commonly euthanized. Puppies are generally vaccinated at 12 weeks of age, and then annually. Although rabies is on the decline in the world community, tens of

This pack of Great Danes contemplates crossing a creek. Remember that the Great Dane has a short coat and during the winter months his outdoor activities should be lessened.

ISABELLE FRANCAIS

people through wildlife: in North America, principally through the skunk, fox and raccoon; the bat is not the culprit it was once thought to be. Likewise, the common image of the rabid dog foaming at the mouth with every hair on end is unlikely the truest scenario. A rabid dog exhibits difficulty eating, salivates much and has spells of paralysis and awkwardness. Before a dog reaches this final state, it may experience anxiety, personality changes, irritability and more aggressiveness than is usual.

thousands of humans die each year from rabies-related incidents.

COPING WITH PARASITES

Parasites have clung to our pets for centuries. Despite our modern efforts, fleas still pester our pet's existence, and our own. All dogs itch, and fleas can make even the happiest dog a miserable, scabby mess. The loss of hair and habitual biting and chewing at themselves rank among the annoyances; the nuisances include the passing of tapeworms and the whole family itching through the summer months. A full range of flea-control and elimination products are available at pet shops, and your veterinarian surely has recommendations. Sprays, powders, collars and dips fight fleas from the outside; drops and pills fight the good fight from inside. Discuss the possibilities

dog shows or obedience or field trials). Athletic, active, and hunting dogs are the most likely subjects, though any passing dog can be the host. Remember Lyme disease is passed by tick infestation.

As for internal parasites, worms are potentially dangerous for dogs and people. Roundworms,

A Great Dane and his Doberman Pinscher buddy play a game of fetch in the water.

ISABELLE FRANCAIS

with your vet. Not all products can be used in conjunction with one another, and some dogs may be more sensitive to certain applications than others. The dog's living quarters must be debugged as well as the dog itself. Heavy infestation may require multiple treatments.

Always check your dog for ticks well. Although fleas can be acquired almost anywhere, ticks are more likely to be picked up in heavily treed areas, pastures or other outside grounds (such as

hookworms, whipworms, tapeworms, and heartworms comprise the blightsome party of troublemakers. Deworming puppies begins at around two to three weeks and continues until three months of age. Proper hygienic care of the environment is also important to prevent contamination with roundworm and hookworm eggs. Heartworm preventatives are recommended by most veterinarians, although there are some drawbacks to the regular introduction of poisons into our dogs' systems. These daily or monthly preparations also help regulate most other worms as well. Discuss worming procedures with your veterinarian.

Roundworms pose a great threat to dogs and people. They are found in the intestines of dogs, and can be passed to people through ingestion of feces-contaminated dirt. Roundworm infection can be prevented by not walking dogs in heavy-traffic people areas, by burning feces, and by curbing dogs in a responsible manner. (Of course, in most areas of the country, curbing dogs is the law.) Roundworms are typically passed from the bitch to the litter, and bitches should be treated along with the puppies, even if she tested negative prior to whelping. Generally puppies are treated every two weeks until two months of age.

Hookworms, like roundworms, are also a danger to dogs and people. The hookworm parasite (known as *Ancylostoma caninum*) causes cutaneous larva migrans in people. The eggs of hookworms are passed in feces and become

If your Great Dane has fleas, washing him with a flea shampoo will help to eradicate them. Photo courtesy of Hagen.

infective in shady, sandy areas. The larvae penetrate the skin of the dog, and the dog subsequently becomes infected. When swallowed, these parasites affect the intestines, lungs, windpipe, and the whole digestive system. Infected dogs suffer from anemia and lose large amounts of blood in the places where the worms latch onto the dog's intestines, etc.

Although infrequently passed to humans, whipworms are cited as one of the most common parasites in America. These elongated worms affect the intestines of the dog, where they latch on, and cause colic upset or diarrhea. Unless identified in stools passed, whipworms are difficult to diagnose. Adult worms can be eliminated more consistently than the larvae, since whipworms live unusual life cycles. Proper hygienic care of outdoor grounds is critical to the avoidance of these harmful parasites.

Tapeworms are carried by fleas, and enter the dog when the dog swallows the flea. Humans can acquire tapeworms in the same way, though we are less likely to swallow fleas than dogs arc. Recent studies have shown that certain rodents and other wild animals have been infected with tapeworms, and dogs can be affected by catching and/or eating these other animals. Of course, outdoor hunting dogs and terriers are more likely to be infected in this way than are your typical house dog or non-motivated hound. Treatment for tapeworm

dog's bloodstream when bitten by an infected mosquito. The larvae take about six months to mature. Infected dogs suffer from weight loss, appetite loss, chronic coughing and general fatigue. Not all affected dogs show signs of illness right away, and carrier dogs may be affected for years before clinical signs appear. Treatment of heartworm disease has been effective but can be

These Great Danes are serious about good health and proper hygiene.

ROBERT SMITH

has proven very effective, and infected dogs do not show great discomfort or symptoms. When people are infected, however, the liver can be seriously damaged. Proper cleanliness is the best bet against tapeworms.

Heartworm disease is transmitted by mosquitoes and badly affects the lungs, heart and blood vessels of dogs. The larvae of *Dirofilaria immitis* enter the

dangerous also. Prevention as always is the desirable alternative. Ivermectin is the active ingredient in most heartworm preventatives and has proven to be successful. Check with your veterinarian for the preparation best for your dog. Dogs generally begin taking the preventatives at eight months of age, and continue to do so throughout the non-winter months.

ALSO BY TFH PUBLICATIONS, INC.

THE GREAT DANE PS-826
In this practical, beautifully illustrated book—filled with more than 200 full-color photographs—author Anna Katherine Nicholas traces the development of the Great Dane from Germany to other parts of the world; and through numerous kennel stories, she brings to life many of the important Great Danes and their people who have made this breed so special. Whether you are a newcomer to the Dane fancy or have been breeding and exhibiting these handsome dogs for years, there is something for everyone in this fascinating volume.